KING-MAKER

Contents

© March 2022

Publisher

iChangeNations and Every Girl Wins Publishing

Printed in the United States of America

INTRODUCTION

Do you know you are KING? Do you know who you really are? Are you operatinglike one? You'll know what to protect if you know what you are protecting.

Allowing your mind to see what's deep inside you, discovering who you need to protect. Let not your emotions dictate who you are. Remove what you feel and get real with yourself. Take action and defeat retraction from what you think you feel. Humility creates liquidity, which molds you into whatever you want to be, not what the world tells you who you are to be. Ignite the inside to shine outside of you.

When the Lord Jesus Christ gave me this vision, it was an eye opener to me towitness it for my own experience. The Lord inspired me, and I had sleepless nights writing this training manual on how to be a king in my own domain.

My own experience is the perfect example of a King Maker. I had a stroke on March 15, 2020, and the Lord has allowed me to see the difference between a worker of God and a servant of God. I had been involved in working for

God and working through it, I forgot that serving Him is allowing me to be a king not a prince. I was expecting my income and credit scores and overall plans would now go into negative territory. But changing my mindset and allowing Him to show me what is my territory, I saw the big difference in my life. He turned me into a real king. I was able to get a new car, increase my income without exerting any effort, found ministry growth, my credit score shot up, acquired a Doctorate degree, a Chaplain and became a Professor while in this condition. It is all because changing my mindset into a king mindset by knowing my territory, how I'm able to manage the territory and the authority and leadership while managing the territory.

You create your own world from your mind. Don't let the world create you. If the world creates you, the world wins, it will own you. You have to be the one to change your world. There are 7.8 billion people in the world, but there are only 2-percent that really have a definite mindset. This series will unravel the big mystery that is in you that the world will be scared about. There are also 20 billion people that have died in the last 6000 years. There is only less than 1% that left something for us as their legacy.

This book is focused on the real you that is screaming and wanting to be the leader, but this is not for everyone. You have to remove the religion, scientifics, statistics, and human reasoning that you learned. This deals with the original intent of life. Life is not living to be number one and be alone on the top, but living for others to share.

If you only knew that what you lost means you already have it, but it has fallen. Do you know what you lost? The only thing is you don't know what you really lost; you lost dominion or rulership over everything God made for you. And at the same time, you don't know how to maintain; have authority and leadership. What you do is try to lead or control something that is out of your boundaries. It was there for you all along to unveil it. The way to uncover it is to have a humble heart. You have to say to yourself you know nothing and let God fill you with something—many things. The goal is for you to identify your destination. All important aspects in life are to be reclaimed, redeemed, restored, reconciled, renewed, because all this starts with "re," which means repeat, as you really are starting over from the beginning, and it refers to going back what you lost. So what you need to discover is that you own a dominion and rulership of your own territory. Never try to rule other people and their dominion, as it's a waste of your time and you never had control over it in the first place.

Understanding the words "I am." When King Jesus identifies Himself, He puts it into perspective, where "I am" too. I need to focus on my own change, not changing others. Don't subject yourself in the affairs of other successes or failures, just focus on you. That word is powerful and full of subjective purpose, yet people miss it. What defines a person is himself. Who can define it? Not others, as I have learned that lesson a long time ago. No one knows you better than you. I love me, the way God designed me, as I can only depend on me and God in this world, and God has given me territory, authority, and power.

If a project is stressful and it's not yet a clear instruction from God, I wait until He gives me the full plan, then go ahead with it. I have to be a master builder to maintain and manage it. I have to have a blueprint where everything is laid out before executing it. When the Lord instructed Noah to build the ark, he gave a blueprint on how to build it.

This program will allow you to identify your territory, explain how to maintain your territory, and instruct on how to have full authority and leadership. It will allow you to be trained in how you can grow in kingship through this program.

The objective of the church is to equip people and prepare them for daily life. The preacher gives you food for the spirit to eat, but it's up to you to receive it or neglect it. All the scripture that they are throwing at you is all good and gives you insights in how to manage and to have authority in your territory daily. It is only pure information, not transformation. But there is no structure or direct design that they share in making you a king.

Genesis 1:27 So God created man in his own image, in the image of God created **he him**; male and female **created he them**.

This passage is missed by many people as it is indicated that "he" for both male and female. Which equates to you're a king.

If you pay attention, you will dissect what it really means. You will notice God created male and female and called them he. Notice the "he" part for both male and female. Meaning that you are a king even though you are female. King means ruler. He made you a ruler, not just a title. In the eyes of God, you are a king, no matter your gender. The name Adam is derived from the Hebrew word "mankind," which is the universal name for male or female, non-gender specific.

Revelation 18:7 How much she hath glorified herself, and lived deliciously, so much torment and sorrow give her: for she saith in her heart, **I sit a queen**, and am no widow, and shall see no sorrow.

If you look at the passage closely, the Queen is the soul and the king is the spirit, as you are a spirit that has a soul that lives in the body. Even if you look at your body as male or female, which is your outside appearance, your soul is a queen in you. The way to look at this is how you live right now; if you glorify yourself and the only important being is you. He is the King of kings and the Lord of lords, and we shall reign with Him here on earth forever. While we are here living in the temporary world, we are a king, and He was made as king and ruler of our own territory.

Revelation 5:10 And hast made us unto our God **kings and priests**: and we shall reign on the earth.

And the last aspect is we don't till the land, we maintain it. Don't just read this book and don't do anything, or else this is just information, not a transformation for you to maintain. A friend of mine told me, I still need to do something for me to have what I have, but I told him yes but not the "do." You expect that I need to do hard work. It is so easy and effortless, as I know how to do it by learning and acting on the kingship principles. Hard work for many people is to put in all that you have until you sweat, but I say work smart and you will come out ahead and tirelessly accomplish the task at hand in no time.

Genesis 3:23 Therefore the Lord God sent him forth from the garden of Eden, to **till the ground** from whence he was taken.

Sometimes, you think that other people have more than you have because they are better than you. It is true in a sense of comparing yourself to them rather than looking at yourself and transforming you to a better you. No one is better than the other, as we are designed unique in the eyes of God. Don't ever look at others like you want to be like them, then you will work hard and find out you are not them.

Like Michael Jordan, it doesn't mean if you wear his shoes you will be like him, fly like him, or shoot like him. What you want is to be like you, not like Mike.

You work hard and sometimes have sleepless nights, you feel just have to finish what you ought to get done. What if you are dead before the deadline? What if you got sick and now all your hard earned money has to go to hospital bills? All that hard work for nothing because you are tilling the land. Don't let your mind get ahead of yourself. Always just take one day at a time. Don't take tilling the land literally, it just means hard word or working hard.

And the curse from God was removed after Noah's flood.

Genesis 8:21 And the Lord smelled a sweet savour, and the Lord said in his heart, I will not again curse the ground any more for man's sake; for the imagination of man's heart is evil from his youth; neither will I again smite any more everything living, as I have done.

The curse is no more, but man still tills the ground. It is never removed from the subconscious mind, or shall I say heart, from generation to generation. You have to reprogram your subconscious mind into unfolding and uncovering the real you. God sees you beautifully and wonderfully made. But whenever you look at a mirror, you don't see it, because you are seeing the outer man, not the real man in you.

So, there you have it. You have inside of you something that no one knows about you, but now it's time! You are a king, you maintain the territory, and the Queen is your soul, but you are not to till any territory!

King-Maker - Part 1

First, let us establish why you get to be a king. You have to be a believer of Jesus Christ and follower, or else do not proceed, as you can't be a king. This is only for people who are followers of Jesus Christ. But if you want to learn of being a king, read on. Becoming a follower of King Jesus is to do what He did while He was here on earth. Second, is King Jesus was crucified on the cross as a king and died for the world. King Jesus told Pontius Pilate, His kingdom is not of this world. Now when King Jesus died, He resurrected and will reign with the kings on earth. Now if He is a king, He has to die for us to be placed as kings on earth in our own territory.

Kings are abiding by the law they create. The law is good, and it should be followed and abided by. Each law has consequences and penalties. The law makes the operation of a king easy, but not easy when it comes to implementing it. God gave the law so that you don't fall into anything that is not in your territory.

What is My Territory?

We are very protective when it comes to our own personal ownership. And if it's not attached to us, it's like something is missing. One example is your cell phone, if it's not close to you, you'll feel like you will miss a message or two. The sense of seeing it and controlling it gives you a sense of security. This is similar to your territory.

Territory- an area of land under the jurisdiction of a ruler or state.

A territory is the area that you see and control. Things that are not in your control are not your territory. You are in charge of your territory, no one else. It is something that is shared with others, except it is only yours alone. Examples are: sickness, relationship brokenness, financial instability, and events that are out of your control. These things that are beyond your comprehension are not your territory.

Genesis 1:26

And God said, Let us make man in our image, after our likeness: and let them have dominion over the fish of the sea, and over the fowl of the air, and over the cattle, and over all the earth, and over every creeping thing that creepeth upon theearth.

When God says let us have dominion over all and upon the earth, it means everything we see and that is in our control. You need to understand what dominion is and the things that you see. We don't control people, we work with people. Everyone has their own dominion. But if you are not focusing on your own territory, you will always make the mistake of controlling what is outside of your lane or boundary. Stay in your own lane. Focus on your own growth. Other people are so used to having opinions of others. They want to know other peoples' business rather than focusing their effort and energy on themselves.

Dominion - sovereignty or control. The territory of a sovereign or government.

You need to identify the things that you have control over in your life and what you see. The things that are not in your control means, it is not your job to control it. Jabez prayed that his territory be enlarged.

1 Chronicles 4:10

And Jabez called on the God of Israel, saying, "Oh that Thou wouldest bless me indeed and enlarge my borders, and that Thine hand might be with me and that Thou wouldest keep me from evil, that it may not grieve me!" And God granted him that which he requested.

Jabez means pain. You have to first look at yourself and see that you are broken and the Lord restores you from your original state. Jabez is coming from the understanding that the territory he has does not come from him. The original territory is not his, and out of the brokenness, God gave him to have a territory. Understanding the territory is given to you by God is a big thing, as it was not yours from the very beginning.

That means Jabez has a clear understanding of what his territory is. That is why the Lord enlarges it. You need to understand your territory first before He can increase what you already have. Whatever you have now cannot grow without knowing that faithfully you can manage it.

Enlarging your territory is not for you but to His glory. When you ask for your territory, you have to keep in mind it is for His glory. We don't want to ask and maintain your territory for your own sake, but it is for people to see who gave it to you and who will be glorified.

Our walk must be trust and obey, there is no other way. Thy will be done. His will, His bill. His way, just obey. Doing what He commands us in obedience, not grumbling or murmuring. Philippians 2:14 Do all things without murmurings and disputing. When God ask us to pray, His will be done, He meant for your final destination will be done. We are still in control of what needs to happen on earth. That is why it is called 'partnership' with God. Because He gave us free will to choose, God never forced anybody, He is directing our path, but at the end of the day, the end result, His will be done.

Deuteronomy 19:8-9 8 And if the Lord thy God enlarge thy coast, as he hath sworn unto thy fathers, and give thee all the land which he promised to give unto thy fathers; 9 If thou shalt keep all these commandments to do them, which I command thee this day, to love the Lord thy God, and to walk ever in his ways; then shalt thou add three cities more for thee, beside these three:

It is very clear that the King has to enlarge your territory, as long as you love the Lord your God with all your heart, soul, and strength and walk in the way He prepared for you. There are many people today who say they are walking in His ways, but you will know them by their fruit. The fruit of the Holy Spirit is not just there to display the one that comes out from you, but it is there to be you!

You are from prince to a king. You used to be a prince, but since King Jesus died on the cross for you as a King and Father, you are now a king of your own territory. You have to realize that you are always in training. And you need to be trustworthy of the territory that He has given you. There is a saying: faithful over little and ruler over much.

You have to say to yourselves, 'I am a king in my own domain and territory.' You have to be faithful first over little, then He will make you ruler over much. We have to have an understanding first of where to start, where to begin. It is mind blowing when you ask people if they know their territory, then when chaos hits the territory they think is theirs is not even it. You have to identify your territory in order to manage it correctly. You need to also look at your own backyard.

Matthew 25:21

His lord said unto him, Well done, thou good and faithful servant: thou hast been faithful over a few things, I will make thee ruler over many things: enter thou into the joy of thy lord.

Image and Likeness - Can be Translated to Relationship and Fellowship

We are built for relationships and fellowship. Relationship with God is very important, we should know where the source is coming from. We need to be connected with the source first before we can have a fellowship with others. Fellowship means getting along with everyone. You have to see everyone is created to conform in His image and likeness. This means God loves everyone; so, should you, especially the ones that you hate. You need to be like God, as He created you the same as Him. It should not be picking whom you want to love and only the ones that get along with you.

We conform to the image of His Son.

Romans 8:29 For whom he did fore know, he also did predestinate *to be* conformed to the **image of his Son**, that he might be the firstborn among many brethren.

Genesis 1:27 So God created man in his own image, in the image of God created he him; male and female created he them.

So, you have to look at this territorial aspect in spiritual eyes, or else you will miss it. Don't be deceived with what you see or what you know. It has to be seen in the spirit.

If you look at the things carnally, you will miss it and you won't understand the real territory and managing it. We always have to remind ourselves that **we are a spirit that has a soul that lives in the body**. Having to understand that you're operating from the spiritual being, which is not carnal, not religion, but it's really seeing that everything you see physically is not real.

The territory has to be led and managed from within. It needs to be carefully examined so that you are approved.

Timothy 2:15 Study to shew thyself approved unto God, a workman that needeth not to be ashamed, rightly dividing the word of truth.

It is about understanding the word of truth by rightly dividing it and placing it in our mind. Reading the word is to place it as a decree and a mandate by a king. Allowing yourself to identify with it and by reading it in the right context, it will have an impact in your mind. We always have to examine our mind if we are fit to be a king. The word of truth is to be rightly divided in our mindset of spirit, as there are so-called "bible scholars" who use terminology and words that are fluttering but empty.

The spirit being has to always take over, which you need to be and to know that you have been transformed into the thinking mindset of Christ. And I keep saying this is love from God.

Ephesians 6:23 Peace be to the brethren, and love with faith, from God the Father and the Lord Jesus Christ.

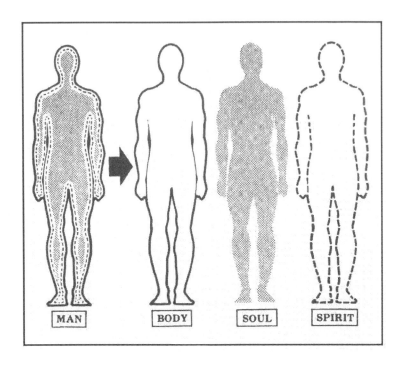

You are a spirit that has the king mentality, as you have the mind of Christ.

1 Corinthians 2:16 For who hath known the mind of the Lord, that he may instruct him? but we have the mind of Christ. The mind of Christ is in your belief system. Not the world belief system but the king's mindset.

The mind of Christ:

1) Sharper then the wisdom of man

2) Once hidden now it's revealed

3) Only given to believers

4) Cannot be understood with the leading of the Holy Spirit

5) Discernment in spiritual matters.

Being a king has to deal with your mindset first. We need to reprogram your belief system into God's mindset, not worldly thinking. Let us start it with your mind system, as your thoughts are not His thoughts.

Isaiah 55:8-9 8 For my thoughts are not your thoughts, neither are your ways my ways, saith the Lord. 9 For as the heavens are higher than the earth, so are my ways higher than your ways, and my thoughts than your thoughts.

The belief system of what you know and have accumulated since you are born, the good and the bad are stored in your mind. It will only be activated on the foreground whenever it is needed. But God gave us a new heart.

Ezekiel 36:26 A new heart also will I give you, and a new spirit will I put within you: and I will take away the stony heart out of your flesh, and I will give you a heart of flesh.

God gave you a heart surgery without you knowing it. He has given you a new belief system that is not of this world. It is from above. Then your thoughts and ways will be different without you knowing it. Your thoughts and ways will never be in sync if you are not allowing His will to be done in your life. Like before we start our day, we should be asking God His will be done that day. The prayer template He taught us.

Matthew 6:10 Thy kingdom come, Thy will be done on earth, as it is in heaven.

The King has to be aligned in His kingdom so that His will be done. You need to understand that the spirit mindset will be aligned and ready to take instructions from the King Himself. We are in partnership with Him.

The Spirit

You need to understand that when you look into the mirror, you won't see the real you, the real king is hidden in you. You are a spirit being, and the one in the mirror is the body that you are residing in. What you need to see is how you will operate from within that body, which is the spirit.

As a spirit, you need to know the component of it:

1) The power

2) The purpose

3) The truth

4) The emotions of God

5) The light

Each part of you represents the real you. But the problem today is we are not seeing it, that is why we are not operating in it.

He gave us the power to be called the sons of God, we need to really see that you are the child of God. And if you are the child of a king, then you should be a king, as He died on the cross for you. That made you a king on your own domain.

John 1:12 But as many as received him, to them gave he power to become the sons of God, even to them that believe in his name:

With that power, He also gave us power from the Holy Ghost to be a witness to the world. To be a witness means He gave us ability and potential.

Acts 1:8 But ye shall receive power, after that the Holy Ghost is come upon you: and ye shall be witnesses unto me both in Jerusalem, and in all Judaea, and in Samaria, and unto the uttermost part of the earth. You already possess that power.

But religion prevents that from being revealed and exposed. He already has ordained you to be the power, but we still ask for it. How can He give you what you already possess?

He also made you a purpose. Not just to have a purpose, but yourself is a purpose. We need to get in touch with our true self in order to find and discover that purpose. Finding one's self is not easy when you are busy with the world. You need to rest and be still for His instructions. Knowing the purpose is to set your mind in His will and just obey without any doubts or questions. Very few people listen to His will and later on find out that they should have done it in the first place.

Romans 8:28 And we know that all things work together for good to them that love God, to them who are the called according to his purpose.

You are a purpose that God intended to be. To everything that He created, you are different and unique, as your purpose changes. The winter goose does not migrate during summertime, they do only in winter. The salmon migrate upstream and never downstream. But with humans, we do change anytime and every time. And during those times, the purpose always changes too.

The term 'the truth shall make you free; is true and fact. Finding the real you is a fact, you are a king on your own domain. The only way is to change from the worldly thinking mindset to the spirit mindset. That is why learning His word of Truth is vital.

John 17:17 Sanctify them through thy truth: thy word is truth.

May God Himself sanctify you, through and through. You have to read His word daily, not only when you need Him to rescue you.

2 Timothy 3:16 All Scripture is God-breathed and is useful for teaching, rebuking, correcting, and training in righteousness,

You are the truth. If you walk in the spirit, you are to correct, rebuke, teach, or edify your brother. You are also being corrected as well, as He chastises the ones he loves. Once you are corrected, it will show in the results of your actions. And people will see the difference in you. No need to brag about it, as it will show or display by your fruit.

The emotions of God are different from our emotions. The real emotions are from God. The emotions of God are genuine, holy, and true. These emotions are from our spirit. You would feel compassionate or kind toward people, or you can be kind without any conditions, as it is unconditional.

And of course, if you are the light of the world, that cannot be hidden. You need to display your character and your value as a King. Don't hide it. A lot of religious people will hide it as humbleness and will never allow the Holy Spirit to manifest in them. When the Holy Spirit is leading you to shine, then shine.

Now Let us Define the Mindset into 3 Different Parts:

6) Conscious

7) Subconscious

8) Unconscious

This 3 are very important, they play a vital role as these are the control system of your body, and how you operate.

The role of the **conscious mind** is everything that you are aware of. It is mental processing; we think and rationalize. The conscious mind includes such things as our sensations, perceptions, memories, feelings, and fantasies inside our current awareness. Everything around us can be thought of, but your conscious mind needs to be focused on it. The conscious mind is the central thinking we use when we are awake and aware. If there are thousands of butterflies around you, your mind will instantly say, it's a lot of butterflies. Now as soon as you focus your mind on one particular thing, then you will describe that specific butterfly and no longer look at all of them. Whenever you are mindful and focus on something, you're using your conscious mind.

The **subconscious mind** also refers to the preconscious mind. It also includes the things that we are not aware of that are just stored in our memory, we can pull into conscious awareness when needed. Subconscious acts as a sort of gatekeeper between the conscious and unconscious parts of the mind. It allows only certain pieces of information to pass through and enter conscious awareness. It is only the storage area. That is why you need to make sure you guard it as the first thing you think of is in the higher level of your subconscious mind. This refers to the heart. The heart is your subconscious mind. If you imagine a glass that has water in it, then pour olive oil into it, the olive oil will float above it, and that's what goes out first when your conscious mind requires information. That is why in radical or quick thinking, whatever the subconscious mind floats first will be the one to carry out first. That is why the Bible says, out of the abundance of the heart, the mouth speaks. That is why reading books allows our subconscious mind to keep storing the higher value of mental thinking rather than the one used on the streets. We need to watch what we are storing in the subconscious mind, especially before going to sleep.

The **unconscious mind** is the things we do unaware that the mind is telling us to do, not knowing we do it. The unconscious mind has an influence on conscious awareness. Sometimes information from the subconscious mind surfaces in unexpected ways, like in dreams or in accidental slips of the tongue. But the unconscious mind is always in reliance of the subconscious mind. So make sure you have your subconscious mind programmed to only store things that are good and acceptable to society, or else you might end up speaking words accidentally that are not in the right manner.

The mind is powerful, and every issue of life flows from it. If you think you will never get ahead, then you won't. We need to understand this thought process, as it affects us being King. We need to practice and keep practicing until we get it. It is not easy to remove old habits and replace them with new ones. One example is getting up early in the morning, if you are not a morning person to begin with.

There is research done that it takes 66 days for humans to adapt to new habits. Until you don't notice you doing it, stay at it.

4th Dimensional Thinking

If you are thinking of the past, present, and future, your mindset is in the 3rd dimensional setting. You are making decisions based on your emotions and your 5 sensory feelings such as touch, smell, hearing, sight and taste.

To follow Christ is to:

1) Slap on the left give the right
2) Lend to someone then forget it
3) Forgive someone that hurt you
4) Pray for those who persecute you

5) Bless those who curse you

6) Sell everything

That list is not the normal thinking of every man. For them it is tooth for a tooth. Live by the sword, die by the sword. But for the kingship perspective of the fourth dimensional mind, it is completely the opposite.

The first dimension is your present situation, the second dimension is your past experiences, the third is your future plans and goals, and the fourth is combining the present with the future. But the first three dimensions set the stage. In the fourth dimension, all things don't exist, you create it from the unseen world to the seen world and speak of things as though they exist.

The inner conversation must take place with you and the helper, which is the Holy Spirit. Those conversations that take place will be in sync with your conscious mind from your subconscious mind. Which are all taking place from the invisible to the visible. You create and finish it all first in your mind before creating it into the world you live in now.

Romans 1:20 For the invisible things of him from the creation of the world are clearly seen, being understood by the things that are made, even his eternal power and Godhead; so that they are without excuse:

Romans 4:17(As it is written, I have made thee a father of many nations,) before him whom he believed, even God, who quickeneth the dead, and calleth those things which be not as though they were.

We need to operate from the unseen world to the seen world. Always be mindful we have a partnership, as God wants to be part of everything we do. **God will not do without man**, and **man cannot do without God**. The ordinary waking consciousness is governed by senses, but the controlled imagination is governed by desires. We need to be operating in our spirit, as it's the place of holies of holy. We need to get instruction from the Holy Spirit of which things to follow and obey.

We need radical mind thinking. The carnal mind has the flesh, normal language, and the mind of Christ as spiritual language. You are unconsciously doing things that you won't understand yet it is happening right before your eyes.

Practice this thinking, as you are the King of your own domain. And the King must not think as the world thinks. To have this mind is to go into a mental diet. When you try to lose weight, you won't eat junk and unnecessary food in your body. Same thing with feeding your mind, filter what is coming into it. Allowing only the things that can enrich and make you grow in wisdom and understanding.

The fourth dimensional thinking:

1. All things are perfect and complete

2. Ethos enabled system (Thy will be done)

3. Always something new in you and around you

4. Always positive even when bad things are happening

5. Boost your mood above feelings

When you go into this different dimension of realization, you are always thinking that it is perfect and complete. Ethos belief is persuaded into believing that it is the will of the Father to direct you into His intentions, rather than having your own reasoning. There is always something new in you and around you every day.

Everything that you do has something to do with you. Whatever is happening around you, always take notice that it is going to affect you, so make sure you guard your mind. When bad things are happening, take a deep breath and say to yourself, 'something good will come out of this.' This will develop your full body to respond to different moods and feelings.

King Jesus established his conscious mind to be focused on his Father's business, which he labors to imitate his Father, to master the Word, master his inner talking, the word He spoke are not his but the Father's through his THOUGHT.

The kingdom's thinking transcends time, space, and everything that is tangible and intangible. Your thinking must be inside the kingdom mindset. It's developing from within where it is being done before the world manifests from within you. Incredible things happen when you set your fourth dimension mindset.

Whoever He makes free, he is free indeed. If God said he made you free from prison, you are given a Kingship title, you need to know exactly what your territory is, maintain, rule, and have leadership. Without knowing this, you are a King but still used to being a slave. Your prison is your mindset. God gave you a new mind to show the true territory to rule. There has to be transformation from within you.

Training 1:

Practice telling yourself for a week, every hour—you are a spirit being and operating in the spirit ,and you are moving in the spirit all day.

Once you master that in your conscious and subconscious mind, all will become natural from you. But of course, at first it will be strange and difficult. Remember you are a product of God. He made you to be the representative of the Kingdom. So this means, He shall supply all your needs

Philippians 4:19 But my God shall supply all your needs according to his riches in glory by Christ Jesus.

He is rich in glory and His check is blank so you can draw any amount and withdraw anytime and anywhere. He needs to make sure He looks good, so He has to make sure you look good as you represent Him. You have to operate from the unseen to the seen world. Meaning you have to think about it in the spiritual mindset, and then you do it to the soul and flesh operation. You will not be able to operate in a King mindset if you're driven by emotions. You will never get to your destination if your emotions are in the way. For example, you see a person walking toward you angry, what should you be showing? He is unseen, and therefore you have to communicate to Him in the mind, which is also unseen. The mindset you have to have is to always be humble. Bowing down to the King of kings and the Lord of lords. His Majesty has to rule your mind and encapsulate your thinking with His words. His words are decree. In order for you to operate the territory, the decree is in your belief system all the time. The belief system is your mind. The more understanding of the decree, the more your belief system increase

The more we read the Bible the more truth we acquire. We should trash all understanding and knowledge we acquire in the worldly view but adopt a new belief system based on the word of truth from the Holy Spirit. The knowledge we received from the Holy Spirit will be embedded in our belief system and we keep on receiving it from the truth.

John 14:6 Jesus saith unto him, I am the way, **the truth**, and the life: no man cometh unto the Father, but by me.

Regardless of whether you are disabled or able-bodied, even blind or deaf, you have a territory, but you have to know and understand is how to operate in it. There are 7.8 billion people in this world, and each has been given territory to manage. Everyone has territory. Everyone has a unique fingerprint, that means everyone is unique.

That is why it is very important that we walk in the Spirit not by the flesh.

Galatians 5:16-18 16 This I say then, Walk in the Spirit, and ye shall not fulfil the lust of the flesh. 17 For the flesh lusteth against the Spirit, and the Spirit against the flesh: and these are contrary one to the other: so that ye cannot do the things that ye would. 18 But if ye be led by the Spirit, ye are not under the law.

Imagine a soldier walking side by side in a straight line along with other soldiers, they look to the right because they need to align with the squad leader, who is guiding them, which Paul says, follow me as I follow Christ. (1 Corinthians 11:1) We need to have a mentor, and someone will be able to look up to. You can't just be on your own doing it without having someone to pattern your life after. Having a mentor does not really mean they will supervise you, it just means you have someone to ask if you are stuck on your decision or advice. To be guided by someone who has been through it and resolved the issues without you going through it is better than just doing it alone and finding in the end you could have avoided it.

These are the Territories We Need to Know

1) ***Your Body*** –

1 Corinthians 6:19 What? know ye not that your body is the temple of the Holy Ghost which is in you, which ye have of God, and ye arenot your own?

It is very important that you know your body before you can manage the other territory. It is the temple of the Holy Spirit. You need to see your body as a vessel, it's only a placeholder of you, a spirit being. So whatever the shape or height of your body, it is what God gave you to manage. That is why He is clear when He says:

1 Corinthians 6:12-13 12 All things are lawful unto me, but all things are not expedient: all things are lawful for me, but I will not be brought under the power of any.13 Meats for the belly, and the belly for meats: but God shall destroy both it and

them. Now the body is not for fornication, but for the Lord; and the Lord for the body.

If you do bad things to the temple, you are defiling what the vessel is used for. Everything is lawful for you, you eat and drink anything you want, but is it glorifying God? That is why you should be careful and watchful of what you take into your body. Or even doing anything with your body.

When the body is sick and not healthy, it is now under not your control. It is the time when it is not yours, you have to look at what God is teaching you to have that sickness and why is it happening. Don't look at it as punishment, as if you did something wrong and that is why you are sick. It is something that you have to look at out of your conditions. It is all about testing your faith. Let God take over the things that can't be controlled.

You need to set an example to everyone that stands out and never settles for less, like in the military. When you are in the military you learn how to be tidy and learn discipline. Your integrity and character will show and stand out!

Example: If your body is fit, you are showing people how you maintain your body. People will notice it instantly, as you have a different glow. And when you add the relationship aspect where you have love, joy, patience, and self-control over it, then you can really maintain your body!

2) *Your Wealth* –

If you think you are starting from zero and no territory, you are wrong! You have the plants and the birds and dominion over all that creepeth on the earth. Before God created you, all was made. Your wealth is already in place and ready for you, all you need to do is manage it.

Genesis 2:8 And the Lord God planted a garden eastward in Eden; and there he put the man whom he had formed, Genesis 2:5 And every plant of the field before it was in the earth, and every herb of the field before it grew: for the Lord God had not caused it to rain upon the earth, and there was not a man to till the ground.

No man to maintain and manage it. That is why He created man. To increase or enlarge wealth, you have to reprogram your mind to the new belief system that is coming from Him. You need to have the proper mindset on how to water and manage the land like watering and maintaining the plants.

Job 1:21 Naked came I out of my mother's womb, and naked shall I return thither: the Lord gave, and the Lord hath taken away; blessed be the name of the Lord. The Lord prunes so we can keep increasing. John 15:5-7 I am the vine, ye are the branches: He that abideth in me, and I in him, the same bringeth forth much fruit: for without me ye can do nothing. 6 If a man abide not in me, he is cast forth as a branch, and is withered; and men gather them, and cast them into the fire, and they are burned. 7 If ye abide in me, and my words abide in you, ye shall ask what ye will, and it shall be done unto you.

You are not to keep the things here on earth but to show how you can maintain and manage what God has given you. You are to bear more fruit so people can pluck some from you. You have to be the role model that the Lord wants you to be.

Your Wealth Territory is Also

1) Spiritual wealth - knowledge, wisdom, and understanding

2) Influential wealth - social, community, and generational

Spiritual Wealth is attainable and can only be learned by the master teaching Himself, the Holy Spirit. In order for knowledge and wisdom to be poured out you have to have the understanding that the teaching and our guide is the Holy Spirit. The worldly teaching is not the institution we should learn from, but from the master of the institution.

Influential wealth is attained by how we relate to people. You should be personable and approachable. An introverted person will not gain access to anything. You need to set up your communication skills to a standard where it needs to be open and able to receive.

Other Wealth Territory Examples:

1) Work - when you know how to deal with your co-workers with love and understanding, the right protocol, you are managing your territoryvery well. Let's say you have a nagging boss or employee, how you deal with them with love is how you can win them. And when you win them over, your work environment will take care of you by getting paid higher or promotions.

2) Car and House - If you know your car needs an oil change, don't you go and do an overall maintenance with it? The

house you live in; it's when you keep it clean and in order that it's a relaxingenvironment.

3) Jewelry and Personal Items - By keeping your jewelry in order and clean and tidy you are able to show you are responsible with what theLord has blessed you with.

Health and wealth is what the world sees what we have. Health is your body and wealth is the tangible and intangible you accumulated. Those are in your control and within your boundaries and reach. That is why it's very important to have that mindset that your territory has to deal with health and wealth.

It is easy to miss what managing means when you are not aware that you are a King that manages the territory God has given you. In managing the territory, we need to have a healthy relationship with it and everyone. Both go hand in hand, the territory is clear that we need to just manage it and not till the land. It deals with letting God be God, allowing the faith you have to work through it all. He says it is impossible to please Him without faith. Having to have a good relationship with others shows you also how you manage your territory.

The faith has to come from Him. Knowing our territory also comes from Him. Everything has to come from Him. That is why you need to know that there are no worries. Without Worries (WOW). To renew our mind is to have the WOE (Worship, Obedience and Everything Is God) mindset.

The enemy of the King is there to steal, kill, and destroy. But with Him we have life and abundance. We need to focus our eyes on Him who is the Author and Finisher of our faith. And we live by faith not by sight. All things work together for good to those who love King Jesus for His purpose.

Romans 8:28 And we know that all things work together for good to them that love God, to them who are called according to his purpose.

It is all about faith while living and showing our life to people. Being a King is to display our banner. And that banner is Love! Knowing that every challenge and difficulty is part of life, you can never avoid it, you have to face it head on. Never avoid challenges, as it brings changes in your life. You always have to receive this as a blessing not a curse. Never underestimate, always look at the bright side of things, how you can grow. Don't let your guard down and get tired and be weary of it. Don't throw in the towel, let your faith in God handle your circumstances, and always have the joy and peace from God.

Always remember, your territory cannot exist in your mind if it is not revealed to you by the Holy Spirit. Once the territory is revealed, you now have to take charge of it and own it. And remember, you cannot give what you don't have. Accumulating wealth is to give it to people that need it, as it will increase your territory. Remember, once traits of a King is to give his territory to others. Your lifestyle has to be like Him. We have to be Christ-like if we want to be a King.

1 Corinthians 11:1 Be ye followers of me, even as I also am of Christ. Become a King as He is a King. You are His child.

Protecting Your Territory

Put on the armor of God to protect your territory.

Ephesians 6:11-12 11 Put on the whole armour of God, that ye may be able to stand against the wiles of the devil. 12 For we wrestle not against flesh and blood, but against principalities, against powers, against the rulers of the darkness of this world, against spiritual wickedness in high places.

The territory has to be protected from the enemy, and the only way to do it is by wearing King Jesus. The WORD! We need to be always ready and alert. Sometimes the enemy will give something good and look good and you are easily driven into it, and then you find out later that it's a trap! Don't let the look and feel deceive you. That is why it's important you have the gift of discernment, as we have to discern the spirits around us. The Bible is clear that you will knowthem by their fruit!

The Angels are also there to help us protect our territory. They are there to do the things of God, and yours too. They are commissioned for us to protect our territory.

Psalm 91:11 For he shall give his angels charge over thee, to keep theein all thy ways.

So everywhere we go they are always ready for instruction to hear from us. Have you talked and commissioned your angels regarding your territory? They are also protecting you, even if you are unaware.

Keys to Kingship Territory

1. Learn to see beauty in everything

2. Check your character, your values and integrity

3. Treat others as you treat yourself

4. Do things and finish it

5. Giving is receiving

6. Become a servant

7. Learn and re-learn every day

The King must learn to see beauty in everything and make it more beautiful. In order to do this, your mindset is to rejoice no matter what your circumstance is. It's about thanksgiving in everything. Beauty is in the eyes in the beholder. You are your world; you can't allow anyone to tell you how you should see the world. You need to see the world from your own perspective, seeing it with a peaceful, loving approach is to see the beauty of God's creation.

The character of a King is very important. It is the basis on how people see your value and integrity. You are valuable like a jewel on display and not hidden. You don't change even in your own home or outside the community. Honesty is one key factor of character. It takes complete confidence and trustworthiness in your words to be honest. Treat your words to be genuine and authentic. Never say one thing and do another.

If you want to be treated with respect, you have to do it first. By treating others with kindness and respect, this will reciprocate to you. If it doesn't, it is not up to you to decide their judgement, but at least you did your part. In any kind of conversation, it is necessary as a King to have dignity and always have decency.

Starting on a project is easy, but make sure it is finished first before starting to the next. Don't try to start something and start another one and then start another one. Keep in mind, always finish one then move to the next. Never think you have to do the next because it is necessary. It is only another distraction from what you already have in the oven. Cook what is in the oven first.

It is better to give than to receive, is what you will tend to hear. But you can't give what you don't have. The mind of a King is always set to give, so there is always an increase in his territory. Only give what is in your territory. Remember, you are here to set an example. Many people are keeping wealth for themselves or only give what is overflowing, but if you give even if you have only one penny left, the reward is greater in heaven. Store up your treasures in heaven, for it does not rust.

The kingdom you have is the opposite of the kingdom you think. The kingdom you think is for you being served, the kingdom of God is to serve others. To serve others is the objective of your being here on earth. Even King Jesus says He came to serve not to be served. Serving others is the objective of the King.

By learning every day, you are being renewed every day. When God says you are renewed every day, it means you are increasing in knowledge, understanding, and wisdom from Him. Make sure to learn every day, do not be busy with work and occupied where you can't increase your knowledge. We have a saying, knowledge is power, a King should have power.

Exercises:

1) What is it that you need to remove from your mind that is always there every day and becomes an instant contradiction of the word? Example (porn, drinking, and lusts).

_____

_____

_____

2) What are the things you need to let go of so He can replace it with what He wants you to have?

_____

_____

3) Who are you putting first? God or things or person?

_____

4) Are you sometimes thinking spiritual or sometimes carnal?

_____

5) Who is maintaining and managing your territory?

_____

Workshop Group: Ask each one of you who makes decisions for you and how you react when someone advises you something.

KING-MAKER - PART 2

How do I Maintain My Territory?

Have you considered your car oil being changed? Your bed being made every day after you wake up? Cleaning after you eat? Brushing your teeth after a meal or taking a bath every day? I guess you at least did one, right? Maintaining anything has to do with the thought of wanting things in order or running well.

Genesis 2:15

And the Lord God took the man, and put him into the garden of Eden to **dress it** and to **keep it**.

When He took the man to dress and keep the land, it is a very clear picture we need to have an understanding we don't have to do more than that. But yet, today we don't even know what dress and keep means. We are just busy bodies to make ends meet to get the standard of life.

Dressing - is to make it beautiful or to embellish the land. Make something from the original state to make it more beautiful. God placed the garden that is already beautiful to dress it up more and made it to their likings as pretty as they want.

1 Peter 4:10 - As every man hath received the gift, even so minister the same one to another, as good stewards of the manifold grace of God.

Keeping - is to watch over the land. And while watching the land we are to wait upon the Lord. Isaiah 40:31 But they that wait upon the Lord shall renew their strength; they shall mount up with wings as eagles; they shall run, and not be weary; and they shall walk, and not faint.

The need to dress it is having the understanding and wisdom on how to operate, and we need this tool to do such tasks at hand:

Tool Set of Growing Knowledge and Understanding:

1) Read the word every day

2) Read books in your spare time

3) Learn something new every day

4) Study your own words and action

5) Learn from your decisions

The word of God can be used on two things, one is for yours and the second for others. By growing your mental vocabulary, it increases your territory. And the word is being stored in your subconscious mind. Reading other books also expands different perspectives. Every author has a different angle of stories, which you will discover and uncover their belief system. The mind has to be transformed daily in the understanding of the spirit not the world. By learning something new every day, you increase your understanding of a lot of things. Take notice of your own words and actions, we tend to say the things that are not meant to be said, but we utter it anyway, and it comes out differently and hurts others. We need to study our own words so the next time you can correct yourself. The mind is the main target to grow your understanding in maintaining what God has given you. And we need to master the following and stand guard by the door of your mind. You only allow things that are creative and fruitful so you can multiply. The need for guarding your mind takes filtering on what is good and bad coming in and knowing what to keep and throw away. The mind is also the battleground to defeat the enemy. He, others or even our own selves are planting thoughts and not allowing our thought process to grow, which are not His thoughts.

Isaiah 55:8-9 8 For my thoughts are not your thoughts, neither are your ways my ways, saith the Lord. 9 For as the heavens are higher than the earth, so are my ways higher than your ways, and my thoughts than your thoughts. Kill it right away as it will be dangerous if it goes like weed and it will bring contamination in your brain.

That is why self-control is important to us. The main thing of maintaining your territory is to master it, not just learn it, but master it. Never allow yourself to be mediocre and just enough. You have to master all these aspects and allow yourself to grow every day. I made this mistake before and lost what I have. Now, I'm able to master it and get better at every aspect of it. Be an expert in something rather than master of none.

Things to Master:

1) Mastering your heart

2) Mastering your conversation

3) Mastering your finances

4) Mastering your happiness

5) Mastering your craft

6) Mastering your discipline

7) Mastering your character

Mastering your heart is mastering your emotions, and more importantly, it is how the mind works. The heart is not the center of your body when it comes to your spiritual heart. The heart that you know is the heart that is beating. Let's say you go to the doctor and the doctor says, we have to give you a heart transplant, then the operation is successful. Your physical heart changes, but your real heart or mindset never changes. It deals with your subconscious mind. Having to master your heart will allow you to open a different dimension of mind set. Pay close attention to your emotions, as they can become your thoughts. For example, stress, as you associate it with a physical response to something suppressing you. You quickly associate physical changes to emotional anxiety. You have to reprogram your thinking from not being prepared to being excited. You also have to understand your emotional vocabulary, which describes how you feel, such as stress, depression, anger, failure, sadness, among others. You have to understand your emotions rather than feeling bad or good. You have to identify them distinctly and be able to change your mindset quickly. Each emotion has 2 different results; either positive or negative. Always replace negative emotions with positive by calling that word to a positive vocabulary.

Philippians 4:6-7 Be careful for nothing; but in everything by prayer and supplication with thanksgiving let your requests be made known unto God.7 And the peace of God, which passeth all understanding, shall keep your hearts and minds through Christ Jesus.

One aspect of mastering your heart is also mastering your core beliefs. Your core belief is new, as the old has passed. You are a new creation in Christ Jesus, therefore you are no longer conforming to the world system. The old belief system is no longer valid, and it has to be operating in the kingdom core belief. Your core beliefs are love, joy, peace, patience, gentleness, goodness, faith, meekness, and self-control. These are the key factors where it should be stored in your core belief system. It should be the center of how you operate in the kingdom.

The King always has treasures that are stored in the treasury. It says you store your treasure in heaven. But where is heaven? And when you die, do you get your rewards after? Whereby we are all the same when we go back with Him here on earth, so what does it mean to store and then receive rewards? Where your treasure is, there your heart be also. So, the treasure is in your heart, heaven is in your heart. When King Jesus says repent for the Kingdom of Heaven is near, it is outside, then He breathes on us to have the Kingdom of God within us. So, it is in us, as the kingdom citizen of heaven. You have heaven in you. And the blessings of God are exceedingly rich, that none can compare to what you received while here on earth.

Always place faith and self-control to work to keep earning. Through those two, you will learn how to love your enemies, share the Gospel, win souls for God, endure insults and persecutions, and forgive. At the end of the day, your treasure is your heart ,and the heart is heaven, as He thought how to pray thy will be done on earth as it is in heaven. The things thatyou do on earth are happening in heaven, which is your heart.

Key Verses:

Psalm 37: 4 Delight thyself also in the Lord: and he shall give thee the desires ofthine heart.

Matthew 6: 21 For where your treasure is, there will your heart be also.

Psalm 20: 4 Grant thee according to thine own heart, and fulfil all thy counsel

Mastering your conversation is in the realm of putting yourself on the stage. The stage that you have is every which way you are conversing with people. Owning your stage is having to be heard, even when you don't speak.

Sometimes in conversations you don't need to speak but still have a statement. What you want to convey is you have to have a win in mind. The win is not a celebratory thing that you express to people, it is something that you learn and receive from the conversation. Even when you start your conversation, once you put the eyes and lips to smile, they will experience happiness and gladness, received with open arms.

Key Verse:

Ephesians 4:29 Let no corrupt communication proceed out of your mouth, but that which is good to the use of edifying, that it may minister grace unto the hearers.

Colossians 4:6 Let your speech be always with grace, seasoned with salt, that ye may know how ye ought to answer every man.

Mastering your finances is one of the most important problems right now in theworld. People are spending more than they earn. If you have more money going out than money going in, you should assess your spending. To maintain your finances, you should make money work for you and not the other way around. First, don't live beyond your means. Cut unnecessary expenses and don't go buying things that in return affects your bills. And saving money will not make you money but investing your money can. Like a parable of 10 talents (Luke 19:12-26). Two guys invested their money and the other took and buried his in the ground. And when the master returned and took an account, the two had shown the master increased their investment, and he said, you are faithful over little and now I will give you to rule over much. But for the guy that buried it, it was taken away and he was reprimanded for it.

Key Verse:

Matthew 6:25 Therefore I say unto you, take no thought for your life, what ye shall eat, or what ye shall drink; nor yet for your body, what ye shall put on. Is not the life more than meat, and the body than raiment?

Matthew 6:19 Lay not up for yourselves treasures upon earth, where moth and rust doth corrupt, and where thieves break through and steal:

Mastering your happiness is the number one thing everyone wants to have. You need to find inner happiness, which is joy in your heart. Not the world's temporary happiness but the joy that comes from within. We are not just here to breathe and work and provide for ourselves and our family but to have joy in everyday life.

Maintain your territory with joy and happiness that comes from Him. There is too much chaos and challenges in the world today, and more and more issues to deal with in everyday life. It is part of life, and it's a promise. So, the only thing we can do is look from within and fill yourself with the word of God.

Psalm 28: 7 The Lord is my strength and shield. I trust him with all my heart. He helps me, and my heart is filled with joy. I burst out in songs of thanksgiving.

Key Verse:

Psalm 16:11 Thou wilt shew me the path of life: in thy presence is fulness of joy; at thy right hand there are pleasures for evermore.

Proverbs 16:20 He that handleth a matter wisely shall find good: and whoso trusteth in the Lord, happy is he.

Mastering your craft is to master your gift that God gave you. Once you become His child, you automatically receive a Spiritual Gift. The gift that is special and fits on you. Do not try to imitate anybody, as your gift is yours and only customized to fit you. We need the grace of God bestowed upon us, dressing and keeping it. Each king received gifts of the Holy Spirit to maintain. Each good gift needs to from us, and it has to be used for His glory.

James 1:17 Every good gift and every perfect gift is from above, and cometh down from the Father of lights, with whom is no variableness, neither shadow of turning.

Here are Some Tips to Master Your Craft:

1. Practice until you are natural to gain confidence, keep doing it, be consistent

2. Believe in yourself, invest in yourself

3. Focus on your skill

4. Seek masters and experts

5. Be fearless not fearful

6. Keep learning, obtain knowledge

7. Know the ending

8. Surround yourself with the right people

9. Begin every day with the beginning, keep yourself fresh

10. Be tired of getting poor

11. Make a lot of mistakes so you can learn from your failures. To fail is to sail.

12. Your competition is yourself

13. Be passionate

Don't Fall into this Trap if You Want to Master Your Craft:

1. Don't procrastinate

2. Don't get into something you are not

3. Don't chase money, make money chase you

4. Don't be comfortable where you are at

Key Verse:

Exodus 31: 3 And I have filled him with the spirit of God, in wisdom, and in understanding, and in knowledge, and in all manner of workmanship,

Exodus 35:10 All who are skilled among you are to come and make everything the Lord has commanded: (NIV)

Mastering your discipline is a must, and keep mastering it in your daily walk. Self-discipline is to have self-control. One example is when you make changes in your diet, don't change drastically but change gradually until you get rid of weight that you don't need. You have to find your weakness and change it gradually. Another example is spending money that you don't have. You are spending too much. It has to be a moderate change and discipline. Creating new habits is giving your mind to focus on new things rather than your routine habits. Create an attainable goal that will not force you uncomfortably to change so that later you get tired of doing it and quit without finishing it.

Hebrews 12:11 ESV For the moment all discipline seems painful rather than pleasant, but later it yields the peaceful fruit of righteousness to those who have been trained by it. Rewarding yourself in every milestone you achieve is good, as it marks your territory with what you already accomplished. 1 Corinthians 9:27 ESV But I discipline my body and keep it under control, lest after preaching to others I myself should be disqualified.

Being disciplined means you have consistency and precision in everything you do. You are able to do with result oriented direction that is within the boundaries. Imagine drawing a line and walking in that line until you get to the finish line. That line is serving as your guide to success.

Key Verse:

2 Peter 1:5-8 For this very reason, make every effort to add to your faith goodness; and to goodness, knowledge; 6 and to knowledge, self-control; and to self-control, perseverance; and to perseverance, godliness; 7 and to godliness, mutual affection; and to mutual affection, love. 8 For if you possess these qualities in increasing measure, they will keep you from being ineffective and unproductive in your knowledge of our Lord Jesus Christ. (NIV)

Proverbs 1:3 Their purpose is to teach people to live disciplined and successful lives, to help them do what is right, just, and fair. (NLT)

Mastering your character is the sensitive area that we need to consider, as it deals with inner behavioral aspects on how we act and react to anything. Your character is your integrity displayed into people's eyes, and it reflects on you. You have to guard your character in every word and action.

Proverbs 10:9 Whoever walks in integrity walks securely, but he who makes his ways crooked will be found out.

To walk with integrity is about what you say and do. Let your talk not be corrupted together with your actions. It is so easy to be found in situations that you are not familiar and your character will be tested. Always be reminded that you are not going to be deceived in any of it, as you are a spirit being that needs to be reminded and acting out of the character of God.

Key Verse:

Romans 5: 3-5 We can rejoice, too, when we run into problems and trials, for we know that they help us develop endurance. 4 And endurance develops strength of character, and character strengthens our confident hope of salvation. 5 And this hope will not lead to disappointment. For we know how dearly God loves us, because he has given us the Holy Spirit to fill our hearts with his love.

James 1:2-4 Count it all joy, my brothers, when you meet trials of various kinds, for you know that the testing of your faith produces steadfastness. And let steadfastness have its full effect, that you may be perfect and complete, lacking in nothing. (ESV)

Copy King Jesus as your role model and copy someone who can inspire you and mentor you. As Paul said, follow me as I follow Christ. You have to have a mentor so you can have an example to make a comparison with.

When you fail it is not called failure, until you quit trying. Keep on going no matter how many times it takes to win. Until you accept defeat, failure will always result in success.

Writing makes you think, thinking creates vision, and vision creates mission. It's the visionary who changes the world. The ability to think always keeps you on top, you are the head and not the tail. The body has limitations but the mind does not.

When you have fear, that tells you can't move forward and you accept what is in-front of you. Fear and being scared are two different things, you can defeat both by courage. You can never allow fear in your head, as God did not give you the spirit of fear but of power, love, and a sound mind.

2 Timothy 1:7 For God hath not given us the spirit of fear, but of power and of love and of a sound mind.

Joshua 1:9 Have not I commanded thee? Be strong and of good courage; be not afraid, neither be thou dismayed: for the Lord thy God is with thee whither so ever thou goest.

These three components complete what we need to maintain the territory, but often it is only words and not exercise. We need to be able to be in spirit in order to tap into that promise. We can't just say it but believe and have faith.

False Evidence Appearing Real - sometimes we look at things as though they are real, but yet there is a lot of evidence they are not real. Like the graphic below, you will read it as GOOD TIMES ARE HERE, but when you try to uncover the whole letters, it's not what it really is.

GOOD TIMES ARE HERE

Once you uncover the hidden letters, this is the result:

CQQD TJMFS APF HFPF

We need to focus on this three:

1) Power

2) Love

3) Sound mind

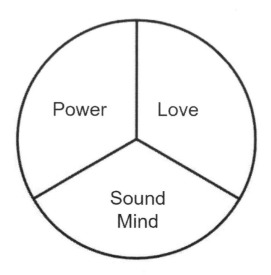

The fullness of our spirituality to protect us from the attack of the enemy is the 3 elements which we have to receive and always be activated. Jesus Christ gave us **power,** but we only know when we activate it, but in everything we do, we have to use the power from Him.

Luke 10:19 Behold, I give unto you power to tread on serpents and scorpions, and over all the power of the enemy: and nothing shall by any means hurt you.

Managing our territory needs to be maintained with power, as we are easily taken aback by our mindset to be easy and taking it lightly. We need to be proactive in all things and mindful of the power He gave us. The Lord has given us power to overcome any fear and have dominion over our territory. Power is always activated in you, as God already gave you that gift. That is instantly engraved into you when you become a King.

Two types of Power:

1) Authority

2) Dunamis (Greek) - potential and abilities

The **Love** he bestowed upon us is the love that no one can fathom, and it's limitless and unconditional. So should we do for others.

James 2:8 If ye fulfil the royal law according to the scripture, Thou shalt love thy neighbor as thyself, ye do well.

It is stated as a royal law and we need to abide by it. The love from God that we have to give and live for everyone to see. By showing forgiveness, compassion and the love for others is how we live together.

Having a **sound mind** is having an active mind. It is not polluted with worldly thinking. It is constantly thinking even when you go to sleep. No matter what you do, your mind never stops thinking, which is to always be in a sound mind.

Your mind is always at war and on the battle ground. So you have to guard and maintain its rootedness to the Holy Spirit.

1 Peter 1:13 Wherefore gird up the loins of your mind, be sober, and hope to the end for the grace that is to be brought unto you at the revelation of Jesus Christ;

You need to know the ending before you begin. Meaning you have to see the ending with a clear picture in your mind to get the real perspective. And knowing the ending, you will know what is needed to get it done.

You have to know your purpose in life for you to maintain it. Without purpose, you are just waking up and doing nothing, as you thought you are maintaining your body or your wealth. Finding your purpose is easy, but you have to know your passion. What you love doing is what you do in everyday life to maintain and keep it. Because purpose gets you out of bed each morning.

Training 2: Eat only healthy food and see how your body reacts. As Daniel, Shadrock, Meshach, and Abednego during their days. Replace watching tv, social media, chatting with friends, doing unnecessary things with working out for 30 minutes a day, or meditate.

Training 3: Remove one habit that you don't like in you.

The body can be programmed by your mind. If you have a stroke or become paralyzed on the left side of the body, the right side will have to do what the left used to do, no matter what. It has to do all the necessary work, and the mind will find a way for the body to function to its fullness. It is amazing that the mind can command the body to operate, not the other way around.

You are not that job, you create a job. Ninety-eight percent of the population are what we call the drifters and do not set their mind to the definite purpose in life.

As we defined, there are 2 parts you need to maintain, which are your own body and your seen wealth.

The reason why you can't maintain is:

1) You are busy.

2) You are lazy.

3) You procrastinate.

4) You keep hesitating.

5) You have many excuses.

Busy like Martha Luke 10:38-42 She became busy with her work rather than being focused and listening to what King Jesus has to say.

Lazy men are soon poor, and hard workers get rich. Proverbs 10:4 He become the poor that dealeth with a slack hand: but the hand of the diligent maketh rich.

Procrastination is that if you wait for the perfect condition, you will never get things done. Ecclesiastes 11:4 ESV He that observeth the wind shall not sow; and he that regardeth the clouds shall not reap.

Thought habits need to be our daily position in life. Once you set up your good habits, then the rhythm of your body will be able to follow and maintain, including wealth. Thought habit is constantly thinking even while you are asleep. Even if you try to close your eyes and not think, you are still thinking, so why not focus your thinking to have the habit of always making yourself grow.

Failure has to be used for our advantage, not negative. Every failure needs to be addressed as testing and perhaps try other routes and do it again.

The key frame that we need to focus on is time and energy. As time will not change but energy will vary in your body and your environment. Environment influences our thought habits, and it gives us perspective on how we should approach things.

Be careful about the influence of the environment, as it can suck you into negative thinking and trap you in that environment. You have to be definite on your decisions and your ways so that you have a change of environment.

Always be aware of the change and once you get control of change then you can adapt your mind to the situation.

Be patient in waiting and keeping your territory as we wait for instruction from God. Patience is key. To take control of your time is to be patient.

Psalm 27:14 Wait on the Lord: be of good courage, and he shall strengthen thine heart: wait, I say, on the Lord.

In Control and Out of Control

a) **In Control** - The things that you can manage and accumulate. These are the things that you need to focus on. In control things are easy to identify but also easy to overlook because we are busy with out of control things. To see this, you need to make a list of things that you are in control of, such as your body, your own accumulated wealth. It's very important to have knowledge and understanding in the field that you want to have a control of.

b) **Out of Control-** From the word itself, the things that you are not in control of are God's job and He and He alone can solve it, and He will do it, no matter what the situation or circumstances are. That is why FAITH is very important to both in and out of control. Especially when things are out of your control. What you don't know will hurt you, and it will automatically give you discomfort. Beyond our control is another term for this, outside of our boundary or territory. You just have to remember—never get out of control.

Maintaining with Wisdom

Wisdom does not come from birth, and it is not acquired but asked, and that comes with authority.

James 1:5 If any of you lack wisdom, let him ask of God, that giveth to all *men* liberally, and upbraideth not; and it shall be given him.

Knowledge is not the same as wisdom, as it is acquired through knowing things.

Change your philosophy in life rather than life changing you. You need to have the perspective of an innovator, inventor, and a motivator. That perspective needs wisdom from God. And wisdom is the application of acquired knowledge and understanding.

Proverbs 10:4 And be not conformed to this world: but be ye transformed by the renewing of your mind, that ye may prove what is that good, and acceptable, and perfect, will of God.

You can alter the course of your life by renewing your mind to the mindset of Christ, using His wisdom, which He gives liberally. Wisdom takes knowledge and understanding, apply it with discernment based on experience, evaluation, and lessons learned. Knowledge is knowing what to say, wisdom is knowing when to say it. Knowledge is knowing a tomato is fruit. Wisdom is knowing not to put it in the fruit salad.

Never use human wisdom as it's earthly wisdom and it's dangerous, as the wisdom from God is spiritual. From the unseen world to the seen world. Don't be fooled with what wisdom you will use, sometimes you see signs and wonders but only find that you end up thinking worldly.

Matthew 16:4 A wicked and adulterous generation seeketh after a sign; and there shall no sign be given unto it, but the sign of the prophet Jonas. And he left them, and departed. It is very clear even the Sadducees and Pharisees have knowledge of the word and are brilliant in worldly but yet they only find wisdom from the world.

When God was pleased with Solomon by building His temple, and the Lord asked Him what kind of reward he wished to receive, he asked for wisdom.

2 Chronicles 1:8-10 8 Solomon answered God, "You have shown great kindness to David my father and have made me king in his place. 9 Now, Lord God, let your promise to my father David be confirmed, for you have made me king over a people who are as numerous as the dust of the earth. 10 Give me wisdom and knowledge, that I may lead these people, for who is able to govern these great people of yours?"

The enemy of God's wisdom is pride. When the pride of life kicks into you, you will not hear what God is telling you. Pride is when you want to hear what you want to hear. Sometimes, the truth hurts and we ignore it. Can you handle the truth?

Overall, to keep and dress the land, you need wisdom from God. Having the power, love, and the sound mind He gave you, and watching and mastering your mind. And upon receiving wisdom, it is all for His glory!

Wisdom from God:

1) Clear your subconscious mind of any known sin

2) Believe the source not others

3) Operate from core belief

4) Desire what He wants not yours

5) Exercise patience

6) Ready and anticipate answers

7) Regardless of answers, just obey

8) Have a sound mind

To have a clean heart, is to have a repentant heart. You clear all your internal motives, replace them with God's motive. Never allow your own understanding and beliefs clutter your mind. Believe in the source and no matter what, don't listen to worldly advice. You will know it's good counsel if it is from the Holy Spirit, which it's light and not heavy in your heart. Make sure you are operating in the core belief, which is the fruit of the Holy Spirit. You have to be aware and ready to receive the wisdom of application. Wisdom applied is wisdom done! The best acronym I can associate with PRIDE is "Personal Responsibility in Delivering Effort." Delivering your own effort is a dangerous thing to do.

Some wisdom applications:

1. Skills

2. Administration

3. Relationship

Being a King, you can apply God's wisdom in the overall aspect of your life. Using your skills and ability, administration, management, and even relationships

Exercises:

1) How do you spend your money? Is it living beyond your means or maintaining it?

_____

_____

2) How are your eating habits? How do you describe it?

_____

_____

3) How do you often work out or go to the gym?

_____

_____

4) How do you balance your budget?

_____

_____

5) How do you intend to grow your money?

_____

_____

Workshop Group: Ask every individual what gift they have and listen to how they apply that gift in their life.

King-Maker - Part 3

How to Have Authority

The word kingdom is a Greek word "basileia," which in turn is a translation of the words "malkuth" (Hebrew) and "malkutha" (Aramaic), which means royal power or to rule. The kingdom is ruled by law. Law gives life. When God created man, He gave the law to abide in it. When God first told Adam do not eat from this tree and if you do you shall surely die, and Satan tricked Eve into eating the forbidden fruit, from then on we lost the rulership and dominion.

You cannot have authority without the law around you being subjected to it. You have been binded by the law in order for you to exercise authority based on that law. You have to ask yourself, where do I receive authority before asking how? Have you known your power but don't know where your authority is? It is very important we understand that authority and that power comes from the law of God and nothing else and the two go together. And then, by reading the manual as a legal document, the Bible, on how to receive authority, you will have an understanding of why there is no such thing as abuse of authority. Are you authorized to do what you do?

Authority - a person or organization having power or control in a particular, typically political or administrative, sphere. A divinely authorized right and responsibility to act on God's behalf from the kingdom authorities of Jesus Christ.

When Adam was asked by God, where are you? God doesn't mean He can't find Adam. He just meant, where is your authority? How come you did not use the authority I gave you? Until this day, some Christian doesn't know their authority and power God gave them. He already equipped you with it, but you don't know you have it. Without understanding His testament as King's, you will read the Bible as religion and you ask for help when you already have it.

Deuteronomy 6: 6-7 And these words, which I command thee this day, shall be in thine heart: And thou shalt teach them diligently unto thy children, and shalt talk of them when thou sittest in thine house, and when thou walkest by the way, and when thou liest down, and when thou risest up.

The law is written in our hearts. It should never depart us, and it is always reminding us we are to abide in it. With authority in the age of uncertainty, we are looking at the world that is corrupt and more uncontrollable. You should not be intimidated by it but be encouraged that you are conditioned for change. Leaders must initiate change and not be intimidated. Fortunately, you do not have to borrow power and authority from anyone as you are using the law of God in every aspect of what you set your mind to.

Adam fell because he did not know his power and authority, but we do because of King Jesus. Without King Jesus, we will still be tilling the ground just as we have always done. When you look at all the prophets sent by God, they always have to hear the word of God before they know what God's plan is. In order for us to have a guide and understanding we have to have King Jesus as the word. When Adam was placed in the garden, named all animals, gave him a woman to celebrate because he found a help meet, and then on top of it all complained and blamed God as to why He gave him these things, all he had to do is dress and keep the land but yet he failed miserably, so how do you expect him to have authority and power over the land.

To keep the land is to watch over the territory that you were given from the enemy who can steal, kill, and destroy. And your authority has to be activated and always on guard.

The soul part of man is one of the enemy of the King. It will try to indulge in the worldly things, as it looks good. That's why Adam can't protect the territory because he too loved the fruit, which he partook in. But you are made from spirit, the Holy Spirit. Which you have to operate from that realm, and that you have authority.

1 Corinthians 15:45 And so it is written, the first man Adam was made a living soul; the last Adam was made a quickening spirit.

But as far as we are concerned, that was way too far now that King Jesus has been given to us to have power and authority with the right mindset. He is the second Adam. Which really shows how the first Adam is a living soul, and King Jesus is made from a life-giving spirit. By accepting Him as your Lord and savior, then instantly you are reborn in spirit and you are now a spirit. A spirit that has a soul that lives in the body.

Mark 11:28-30 28 And say unto him, by what authority doest thou these things? And who gave thee this authority to do these things? 29 And Jesus answered and said unto them, I will also ask of you one question, and answer me, and I will tell you by what authority I do these things. 30 The baptism of John, was it from heaven, or of men? Answer me.

They got a confusing answer as they didn't have a clue. And this passage will answer it clearly:

Matthew 28:18 And Jesus came and spake unto them, saying, all power is given unto me in heaven and in earth.

King Jesus is given power over both heaven and earth. And now, He passed it onto you! We need to understand clearly that the authority and power are already in you. But most Christians ask for power from King Jesus, whereby He already enabled you to have that same power He has to do greater things!

But there are two types of power that we need to understand, one is power in authority to give us the right to be called the child of God. And the other power is ability and potential, which you are built to have a purpose.

The first word you have to understand in authority is **faith**. The key to access heaven is faith. You are in partnership with God. You have to understand, you were given faith to overcome what it is you need to overcome. Without faith it is impossible to finish or to even get started. You will end up staring at it as you fall. Faith is the substance of things we hope for. We need to stand in the good ground, that is where faith comes in. By believing you already have it, you can overcome and conquer. You are more than a conqueror. To meet the issues of life, you have to introduce your faith to it. The faith that no one has except yours. Never compare your faith with others. Faith demands that God is the center and focus of your actions. You believe you are already there, and faith will be your walk to get there.

John 14:12 Verily, verily, I say unto you, He that believeth on me, the works that I do shall **he do also**; and greater works than these shall he do; because I go unto my Father.

Acts 4:7-10 And when they had set them in the midst, they asked, by what power, or by what name, have ye done this?

8 Then Peter, filled with the Holy Ghost, said unto them, Ye rulers of the people, and elders of Israel, 9 If we this day be examined of the good deed done to the impotent man, by what means he is made whole; 10 Be it known unto you all, and to all the people of Israel, that by the name of **Jesus Christ of Nazareth**, whom ye crucified, whom God raised from the dead, even by him doth this man stand here before you whole.

This is Peter when asked by whose power and authority that he was able to do such things. It is by the power of Jesus Christ.

Don't lose your focus on Jesus Christ. Jesus Christ is the word of truth and through Him and by Him we get authority. The legal document that we have, we call it the Bible, is where we should always operate from. This is where we get instructions and directions from daily. We should not be leaning on our own understanding. The words are not powerful without us.

Authority Doesn't Work when:

1) Distracted by circumstances

2) Change of mindset

3) Disobedience

4) Lack of understanding

5) Leaning on our own understanding

When we are distracted and not focused, it is easy to miss the mark. We can't just speak authority out of words, but with power from the word. The mindset has to be set in Christ, as we have the mind of Christ. You have to understand that King Jesus is the Christ. And Christ is a heavenly being and King Jesus is earthly, where human beings can understand, that is why He is the word. Having to have authority is to know how to differentiate and identify the two distinct positions of power. We need to place the two in different areas of our mind. The word is Jesus that we read (graphe), the spoken language becomes the rhema is the Christ. So when we say a prayer we end it with "In Jesus' Name." Meaning, from all what I stand as I said (graphe), I mark it with the word, and let the Chirst (rhema) take over.

The second is the **Word**. The word of God is very important in having authority. Without the word of God, there is no life and power. And of course, when you disobey God, there is no way that your voice will be heard. Some do like to quote the scripture but act the other way. It is easy to be deceived and persuaded by this world. That is why Paul says it straight when he says, I do the things I don't want to do but yet I do them. We rebel against God when we transgress against God. If we are in rebellion and ask for authority, do you think that you will be heard the way you want to be heard? It's like a policeman saying, "I'm doing things against the law, but I will enforce the law on you." You see, it does not align with the scripture.

Authority Over:

1) Me

2) Devil

3) Circumstances (The World)

Devil Can and Cannot do:

1. Cannot read your mind

2. Cannot predict the future

3. Inflict you without permission from God

4. Only read you by your actions

5. Only advice you and cannot revise you

As you move with authority, you should always keep in mind these things that the devil can and cannot do to you. Once you place this in the parameter of your mind, it will become natural to operate without the interference of the enemy. Whatever you put in your mind the devil can only advise what you can and cannot do. No more revision or changes can be done once you execute your actions.

1 John 2:20 But ye have an unction from the Holy One, and ye know all things.

By being called the anointed, you have the authority, so why are you asking God to do something that you already have? You haven been authorized, but you don't even know how. The law is an established principle that everybody needs to abide by. It is the standard that you walk on, and if you break it, you get the penalty for it. An example is gravity. It's already established and if you jump you will come down no matter what. But what law is it that you abide in? Is it the 10 commandments with 613 laws breakdown or the 2 new commandments Jesus gave: love God above all and love others as yourself. These two new commandments are not new, they are just merely summing up all ten, as these ten hang in the two new laws.

Psalm 119:89 For ever, O Lord, thy word is settled in heaven.

When you pray the word is already final and settled, no need to argue about it, just execute it. But it seems that you ask for it as if you have to break the ears of the hearer to be heard. Thy word is settled and final.

Psalm 89:34 My covenant will I not break, nor alter the thing that is gone out of my lips.

His covenant he will not break. How can He break His own word where He already has established it with His written word. All you need to do is believe it.

Psalm 138:2 I will worship toward thy holy temple, and praise thy name for thy loving kindness and for thy truth: for thou hast magnified thy word above all thy name.

His words are true, they will always be true, yesterday, today, and forever. The King of kings has spoken and will never retrieve or backup His word.

Hebrews 1:3 Who being the brightness of his glory, and the express image of his person, and upholding all things by the word of his power, when he had by himself purged our sins, sat down on the right hand of the Majesty on high:

The spoken word has power. Sometimes we associate the two to be the same, as the written word and the spoken word is the same, but they are different from each other. All things are upholding the word by this power.

Training 4: Watch what you say all week. Is it from Him or is it from you?

Fear is not for you. When you have authority, fear should not be in your vocabulary. It should be removed from your mind. The fear of God is different from the fear that we know. The fear of God refers to giving reverence, honor, and glorifying God.

Having to have a gift is having power and authority to do things for others. Spiritual gifts are to exercise your authority in the areas you are placed by God.

Romans 12:6 6 Having then gifts differing according to the grace that is given to us, whether prophecy, let us prophesy according to the proportion of faith;

The third thing is your **gift**. The gift is given to you by God and entrusted to you to edify and exhort God's people. This spiritual gift is according to the measure of faith, which is from him also. Each position has a different obligation to perform. So make sure you know your gifts so you can use them with authority. It's like you are a soldier going to a battle where God prepares you with spiritual gear. The gear you have shows your license is authorized by God.

1 Corinthians 12:4—11 4 Now there are diversities of gifts, but the same Spirit. 5 And there are differences of administrations, but the same Lord.6 And there are

diversities of operations, but it is the same God which worketh all in all. 7 But the manifestation of the Spirit is given to every man to profit with all. 8 For to one is given by the Spirit the word of wisdom; to another the word of knowledge by the same Spirit; 9 To another faith by the same Spirit; to another the gifts of healing by the same Spirit; 10 To another the working of miracles; to another prophecy; to another discerning of spirits; to another diverse kinds of tongues; to another the interpretation of tongues: 11 But all these worketh that one and the selfsame Spirit, dividing to every man severally as he will.

For example, your spiritual gift is pastoring a church, then you have to be fit and mentally prepared before you go out there. Have confidence that you are validated by God. Sometimes we seek approval from man where there are some people that will not conform to God's conformity. We need to learn how to get instruction from Him. There are a lot of pastors that will just copy sermons from others so they have something for that Sunday, but God never approved of it, but they still go with it. Don't be placed in this situation, always ask God what people should receive that day.

When David was about to face Goliath he needed only one stone to kill Goliath. You are always armed with one shot, as our GOD IS ONE. You do not need anyone's approval but God's. Seek counsel if you are in doubt, but God has the final say.

Your spiritual battles are unseen, for we wrestle not with flesh and blood, so God armed us with authority to dismantle and remove it on our way. And when David talked with God, he told Him that he was wrong and confessed his sin of murdering the man and having sex with the woman. By confessing he received merry and grace from God. That's authority exposure. By exposing yourself with God then you will have full authority.

The fourth is **prayer**. Prayer plays a vital role when it comes to your authority. The authority and power with the name of Jesus. Prayer is a petition before a judge that has authority to approve your request. So being a King must know your relationship with the King of kings so your petition is authorized and granted. You have to know your relationship with the Father before He can give you what you are asking.

The Authority of Prayer:

1) God has consistency

2) God gave you dominion

3) Jesus has qualified you

4) Jesus is model of dominion and authority

5) Jesus is ruling through the spirit of Christ.

God is always consistent and always ready to listen to your petitions. There is no traffic or waiting time, you have direct access to Him. You are the apple of His eyes, and He is always focused on you. He already gave you the territory before the foundation of this world, all you need is to uncover your understanding and focus on the things at hand. King Jesus has already validated you and given you full qualification, as you are His representative on earth. The full understanding of what you have is the power and authority coming out of you. Christ is in you, the hope of glory. The glory is you and that glory need not be hidden.

King Jesus demonstrated various authority and power by plants, storms, devil, healing. That's why praying is important, and by praying without ceasing our authority has been validated by Him. And He says this is how we pray.

Matthew 6:5-8 5 And when thou prayest, thou shalt not be as the hypocrites are: for they love to pray standing in the synagogues and in the corners of the streets, that they may be seen of men. Verily I say unto you, they have their reward. 6 But thou, when thou prayest, enter into thy closet, and when thou hast shut thy door, pray to thy Father which is in secret; and thy Father which seeth in secret shall reward thee openly. 7 But when ye pray, use not vain repetitions, as the heathen do: for they think that they shall be heard for their much speaking. 8 Be not ye therefore like unto them: for your Father knoweth what things ye have need of, before ye ask him.

After He us thought how to pray, He gave us a template:

Matthew 6:9-13 9 After this manner therefore pray ye: Our Father which art in heaven, Hallowed be thy name. 10 Thy kingdom come, Thy will be done in earth, as it is in heaven. 11 Give us this day our daily bread. 12 And forgive us our debts, as we forgive our debtors. 13 And lead us not into temptation, but deliver us from evil: For thine is the kingdom, and the power, and the glory, for ever. Amen.

We should be directed properly and orderly when we ask for our petition, as we want to be heard and approved by our judge. If we want our petition to be accepted, we must follow the template and be trained. Because without proper training every word will be meaningless and you have just wasted your time.

The fifth is the **Angels**. Angels are ready to receive instructions from us with authority.

Psalm 91:11-12 11 For he shall give his angels charge over thee, to keep thee in all thy ways. 12 They shall bear thee up in their hands, lest thou dash thy foot against a stone.

Matthew 26:53 Thinkest thou that I cannot now pray to my Father, and he shall presently give me more than twelve legions of angels?

This is when King Jesus was being tried by Pontius Pilate and He was sitting His authority to him. We can do the same, as we need to fight the unseen world, our angels being on our side. Sometimes you feel like giving instruction to someone or God reminds you to call someone, it is better you wait for the right opportunity when He says now. It doesn't mean you give someone instruction and it's not the right time. It has to be God's ordained time and place when you use your authority.

A house divided cannot stand, as the enemy are all united when fighting you. So you need to team up with God as well to obtain authority. When circumstances change it should not change you, but other circumstances change them. You always have to be firm in circumstances when it arises because you will get into it without knowing you are now in it rather than working with it.

Important Value in Authority:

Human equity value - think your ideas are always number one, that no one has heard yet what you are telling them but stay in your lane. Because God has told you but the people have not heard it yet. So when you are sharing your idea, you need to be clear and as precise as God showed it to you. You have to be understandable to be understood, so that your authority will have an impact with your instruction.

Rest in the Lord - as we command without resting, it is impossible to have authority. You need to realize that resting in His presence places you in peace mode, not in beast mode. Understanding the peace and joy value will always put you in focus with the task at hand with the right discipline in mind, as it is easy to be caught up in the busy mode and forget you need to operate in His rest.

Sometimes when things are in your mind, it is easy to derive and arrive on your own drive, not on cruise control where it is controlled by the Holy Spirit. Being controlled by the Holy Spirit is an easy and anointing flow so smooth without exerting efforts.

Listening and Hearing - the best defense is a good offense. Listening, assessing, and knowing the situation before going into the final assumptions gives you great value of our time and energy. The use of time and energy in authority is very crucial if you want to win. In order to have a sense of value you have to learn to listen. Don't jump the gun too soon or else you will learn in the end you made a mistake and fall flat.

King Jesus has Authority Over:

1) The sea

2) The plants and trees

3) The birds

King Jesus has authority over the storm in the sea. He was even sleeping while the boat was being shaken and not even bothered. The storm was so strong, His disciples were worried that they would die from it.

Matthew 8:23—27 23 And when he was entered into a ship, his disciples followed him. 24 And, behold, there arose a great tempest in the sea, insomuch that the ship was covered with the waves: but he was asleep. 25 And his disciples came to him, and awoke him, saying, Lord, save us: we perish. 26 And he saith unto them, Why are ye fearful, O ye of little faith? Then he arose, and rebuked the winds and the sea; and there was a great calm. 27 But the men marveled, saying, What manner of man is this, that even the winds and the sea obey him!

The plant was not bearing fruit so King Jesus commanded it to wither and die. The plant is not fulfilling its purpose. When you are not fulfilling your purpose God is not happy.

Matthew 21:19 And when he saw a fig tree in the way, he came to it, and found nothing thereon, but leaves only, and said unto it, Let no fruit grow on thee henceforward forever. And presently the fig tree withered away.

King Jesus compares man as to the birds and lilies. Man is more well taken care of than birds but leaning on our own understanding leads to tilling the land rather than being dependent on God.

Matthew 6:26 Behold the fowls of the air: for they sow not, neither do they reap, nor gather into barns; yet your heavenly Father feedeth them. Are ye not much better than they?

Matthew 6:28 And why take ye thought for raiment? Consider the lilies of the field, how they grow; they toil not, neither do they spin:

King Jesus demonstrates that everything on the earth you have control and power over. He does it naturally without any effort.

Authority is believing in the scripture, and acting upon the spoken words are the key. Once you know the structure and hierarchy of His instruction, it will have a transformation in you.

Ingredients of Authority:

1) Faith

2) Word

3) Prayer

4) Spiritual Gifts

5) All in power of Jesus Christ

This ingredient when mixed together is like cooking the best recipe that the world has ever tasted. It is through this combination that makes our territory work. If faith without works is dead, then there is no life, but if we mix faith with the word of God with prayer, exposing our spiritual gifts, and overall putting it in the name of Jesus, it will be unstoppable and immovable

Exercise:

1) How do you pray for your people?

_____

_____

2) How can you exercise your authority in times of challenges?

_____

_____

3) If your authority does not work, what do you think you need to do?

_____

_____

4) While praying for others, what kind of result do you expect?

_____

_____

5) What do you think needs to be done to improve your authority?

_____

_____

Workshop Group:

Ask what are your spiritual gifts, how did you know and when did you find out? Engage in how you can combine your spiritual gifts in helping others.

KING-MAKER - PART 4

Leadership

King Jesus gave the order to his disciples to preach the gospel into the world. He gave them not just authority but leadership. Are you a leader that keeps your own rules and abides by them? Are you a leader that only wants authority but not responsibility?

Leadership and management is a completely different and separate approach to maintaining your territory. Management is a group that manages what is established by a leader. It's a system in place where roles are played consistently. It contains the leadership and is placed, then it becomes something where it needs to be managed.

This leadership training is about you as a true child of God. Pay attention and reevaluate your evidence and results to the leadership traits you will discover. The world's leadership is not the same, as you will uncover. It's about responsibility when you become a leader that manages and maintains your territory. The perception of your self needs to be focused on leadership rather than other business. Maintaining, dressing, and keeping the land is a huge task, and leadership is important in how you work within yourself, which is the real assignment from God to us—to take care of the territory. Rulership is equivalent to leadership, it is about serving yourself to rule over your territory and sharing with others the fruit of your labor.

When King Jesus told this parable about 10 servants, He told them they were to engage in business or occupy till He comes. It is showing Adam that he had to dress and keep the land until He comes. And when he returns, he wants to do an accounting of how much of an increase they were able to accumulate, and he will give them rewards. You are to be in charge of your territory before He comes.

Luke *19:11-2711 And as they heard these things, he added and spake a parable, because he was nigh to Jerusalem, and because they thought that the kingdom of God should immediately appear. 12 He said therefore, A certain nobleman went into a far country to receive for himself a kingdom, and to return. 13 And he called his ten servants, and delivered them ten pounds, and said unto them, Occupy till I come. 14 But his citizens hated him, and sent a message after him, saying, We will not have this man to reign over us. 15 And it came to pass, that when he was returned, having received the kingdom, then he commanded these servants to be called unto him, to whom he had given the money, that he might know how much every man had gained by trading. 16 Then came the first, saying, Lord, thy pound hath gained ten pounds. 17 And he said unto him, Well, thou good servant: because thou hast been faithful in a very little, have thou authority over ten cities. 18 And the second came, saying, Lord, thy pound hath gained five pounds. 19 And he said likewise to him, Be thou also over five cities. 20 And another came, saying, Lord, behold, here is thy pound, which I have kept laid up in a napkin: 21 For I feared thee, because thou art an austere man: thou takest up that thou layedst not down, and reapest that thou didst not sow. 22 And he saith unto him, Out of thine own mouth will I judge thee, thou wicked servant. Thou knewest that I was an austere man, taking up that I laid not down, and reaping that I did not sow: 23 Wherefore then gavest not thou my money into the bank, that at my coming I might have required mine own with usury? 24 And he said unto them that stood by, Take from him the pound, and give it to him that hath ten pounds. 25 (And they said unto him,*

Lord, he hath ten pounds.) 26 For I say unto you, That unto every one which hath shall be given; and from him that hath not, even that he hath shall be taken away from him. 27 But those mine enemies, which would not that I should reign over them, bring hither, and slay them before me.

The very first thing you should check is your character and the second is discipline. Character has to deal with your value and integrity, discipline deals with how you operate your character. To put discipline to test, look at your habits. If the habits result is self-centered, then you are operating in a worldly attitude. Confidence in yourself helps you to operate in self-discipline. Having to make a decision of your own is standing for what you believe in, not because of someone else. Self-motivation is a very good attitude and practice of discipline. It really pushes you to make you a better leader. You can't change people, so instead of motivating others, motivate yourself first.

Traits of a Leader:

1) A leader always finishes what they have started. Stop wasting time and cutting corners. You have a finishing spirit. Getting to know how you finish before you start is very important, and it's a must. Never start something that doesn't have an ending. Knowing the clear picture is seeing the total result of what you are trying to build.

Having to have a blueprint and layout of what you are building will give you clear directions and instructions where to start and how to finish.

John 4:34 - King Jesus saith unto them, My meat is to do the will of him that sent me, and to finish his work.

2) A leader has the capacity to influence the surrounding environment based on the mindset of a leader. To influence others, a leader must show credibility and trustworthiness. You must demonstrate that you are worth following. You don't need to impress. All you need to do is focus on the job at hand, be joyful of what you do, and show eagerness to accomplish whatever the task at hand is.

Proverbs 13:20 - He that walketh with wise men shall be wise: but a companion of fools shall be destroyed.

3) A leader is a reader. A reader means to re-add to your knowledge. Spending time reading is to have an open mind to the world. Reading other books is giving your mind to all different possibilities and widening your thinking to other possibilities.

1 Peter 2:2 - As newborn babes, desire the sincere milk of the word, that ye may grow thereby:

4) A leader is not to lead but empower people in finding their passion and vision. Empowering others means putting them in a position of getting better than yourself. As you place them ahead of you and allow them to excel in what they do, it allows you to excel as well. By seeing others improve and become elevated by your help, it speaks more highly about you. It is a selfless act when we want people to do better, and look at what they can do in their own territory.

1 John 4:4

- Ye are of God, little children, and have overcome them: because greater is he that is in you, than he that is in the world.

5) A leader is not looking for fame but to gain influence by being the inspiration. Being an inspiration to others means to show your result of how you live your life. To be an inspiration to others, the life you are living is acceptable to the society and according to the standard placed by society. What is the standard? It is how you become a citizen that loves God and loves others. Walking an

inspired life is always living with love from within and then without.

1 Thessalonians 5:11 - Wherefore comfort yourselves together, and edify one another, even as also ye do.

6) A leader doesn't need to fight with muscle but with brain. He uses his ability to think not only his power but authority. A leader must always think before acting. You have to be calculating in your mind, what will be the outcome before doing things.

Ephesians 3:20 - Now unto him that is able to do exceeding abundantly above all that we ask or think, according to the power that worketh in us.

7) A leader is a visionary and allows everyone to see the same vision and make it a goal. To get to your destination, everyone must know the direction you are going to take. All the participants must know the instructions and the ending of the works. When the vision is clear in your head, let others see it clearly written down in detail.

Proverbs 29:18 - Where there is no vision, the people perish: but he that keepeth the law, happy is he.

8) A leader is focused on the mission not on the emotions. Your journey is an experience and the destination is the result. Never allow your emotions and feelings to affect your decision making. Sometimes, we have to make hard choices that often hurt you or other people. It is better to fix it than to let the brokenness linger until it is too late.

Proverbs 16:32 - He that is slow to anger is better than the mighty; and he that ruleth his spirit than he that taketh a city.

9) A leader is ready to die in their belief system, and has the willingness to abide by it. You have to hang on to what you believe in no matter if people tell you it's wrong. Standing by what you believe in is your ground. Never let anyone persuade you in their own belief, and at the end of the day, you are the one to suffer the consequences. A good leader will always stand by what they see as the right thing to do.

Romans 8:38-39 - For I am persuaded, that neither death, nor life, nor angels, nor principalities, nor powers, nor things present, nor things to come, nor height, nor depth, nor any other creature, shall be able to separate us from the love of God, which is in Christ Jesus our Lord.

10) A leader has been through it and shown the ropes to others; the easier way to do it. He leads you to the top! They say experience is a good teacher. Making lots of mistakes is always good, but as long as you learn from it. Once you learn from it, teach it, so others don't make the same mistakes. Teach them the right path to take, as you already have been through it.

Job 32:7 - I said, Days should speak, and multitude of years should teach wisdom.

11) A leader does not attract followers, but followers are attracted to him. It is said that leaders are doers not just sayers. And when you do, people will take notice of it, and they will be attracted to what you do. Just keep doing what you do best, and keep improving until others see and want to learn from you.

John 7:4 - For there is no man that doeth anything in secret, and he himself seeketh to be known openly. If thou do these things, shew thyself to the world.

12) A leader always looks for successors to do greater things than he, he is passing the baton. When you learn how to create successors, you will also learn promotions. Promotion does not only come from your successor but it

will also benefit you by allowing yourself to grow from one success to the next.

John 14:12 - Verily, verily, I say unto you, He that believeth on me, the works that I do shall he do also; and greater works than these shall he do; because I go unto my Father.

13) A leader is cultivating the gifts and talents of every individual that follows him. Always keep in mind, every talent is needed to get things done. Knowing one talent and ability is knowing what you can build with them. Having to shape one talent is taking advantage of your ability of one already, and all you need to do iscultivate it.

1 Peter 4:10 - As every man hath received the gift, even so minister the same one to another, as good stewards of the manifold grace of God.

The best example for all of this is King Jesus. That's the leadership secrets of KingJesus. He did all this without any hesitation and knew that whoever He trained and followed in His footsteps would do greater things than He did here on earth.

Training 5:

Try to see how you become an influence in your household or community. How do you make an impact in their lives while conducting your own business?

The leader must be trustworthy in his character, ability, credibility, and integrity. All the conviction of a leader comes from belief and moral values. There is no fear of failure but always focus on success. The character of a leader is very important. The character should be shown from both private and public life. If a person wants to be a leader then you are really saying you don't like to be a leader but you are acting as a leader. The character that you possess attracts people who want to be led. You can't lead if you don't show an example. You need to have a verified portfolio, evidence, and results. It shows in your character and your walk in life. Character means one, and one means holy in the Hebrew word. You have to be the same, either in or out of your rooms, wherever you are. The leader is focused on serving others rather than being served.

People don't need to follow you if you are not trustworthy. Your work will speak for itself. A leader doesn't even have to speak but shows their character in the way they stand.

Leaders must know:

1) Know how to delegate

2) Know how to distribute

3) Know how to recognize gifts around them

4) Knows when stop, wait, and go

5) Know who to serve

6) Knows the ending before beginning

The blind leading the blind is a formula for disaster. If your leader is blind how do you expect to get to where you need to be? The blind will always put you in a blind spot! The leaders see the light as he conforms to the image of Jesus Christ. Every man is not in the image of God until they conformed with Jesus Christ.

Romans 8:29 For whom he did foreknow, he also did predestinate to be conformed to the image of his Son, that he might be the firstborn among many brethren.

Fear of God is to respect and to honor. That's the fear of the Lord. Remove fear of the world, but rather fill your hearts with peace and joy with thanksgiving to God. All fear is cast out and the fear of the Lord is cast in. The need for influence is the leader's secret weapon on how we win others. By the power of influence you can transform an individual. Showing to others how it is to live a Christ-like walk. It creates influence and you don't even have to talk. Influence is outside, but your inside needs to do the showing.

How to Create Influence:

1) Show your net worthiness, character, integrity

2) Willing to listen

3) Be interested in what others have to say

4) Engage with edification, empathy, and encouragement in mind

5) Do what you say you will do

6) Get them involved in what they can involve

7) Communicate with clear vision and understanding

The difference between a boss and a leader is the boss is never listening to anyone but themselves. The boss is always right and can never be corrected. The boss will never admit they made a wrong or bad decision. The boss will always push you even when you are weary and tired of work. Boss always demands. They always have the last say and you can never be heard. Bosses manage their employees while a leader inspires them to innovate and think creatively.

The quality of a leader is not the same as the qualification of a leader. A quality means you are born to it and it is embedded in you, and the qualification is how you apply what you already have. In short, a qualification is a guideline. You have the leadership in you but you need to discover and place it in order to show qualification. You have to step out of your comfort zone and see the leader in you. A leader doesn't need validation, except from God. To lead is to show an example and a guide. You are simply displaying a role model to them, like King Jesus did.

Exercise:

1) Look at your daily habits, does it make an impact on people around you?

_____

_____

2) What kind of influence do you impact in your community in terms or your character?

_____

_____

3) Are you giving instructions to your subordinate in clear and concise terms or just letting them do what they have to do to accomplish their task?

_____

_____

4) How do you serve others?

_____

_____

5) Do others feel comfortable working around you?

_____

_____

Conclusions:

What you need to see to uncover the real you is yourself. Picture yourself as having a cape and a rod, ruling your own territory with authority and leadership in mind. Your belief system has to be programmed in knowing who you are and who owns you.

Knowing your boundary and your territory will place your understanding in a broader spectrum of life. Being content means you know what it means to have success in life. Live like a King!

Life is complicated when you allow the world to dictate what you need to feel or do. Take over your kingship and orchestrate the rhythm of your life. Knowing that you are a King makes it a lot easier to live life in any circumstances. Allow your mind to believe and live it, as a demonstration of your territory being managed by a King. Let your imagination from your thoughts be positive, always rebuking the negativity that comes across with your thinking. Take action habits and be good at it. Taking charge of your life is easy when you align your mind with the word of God. Free up your mind from the prison of your own mind by reading the word of God. Never allow anyone to dictate what needs to be done in your territory, as you are to dress and keep watch over the land.

You are life and you make life, as the word says, the word that King Jesus speaks unto you is life and you are the carrier of the word, so you are life. Having the decree and walking in them is being in alignment of the blessing and His will. By comparing your life as a King to another being that is not, you will see the elevation on how you operate and how they live their life.

I hope this book has helped you to see the inside of you. By guiding you to discover other mastery and propel yourself to the next level of your exciting life. Be blessed and always stay blessed.

Made in the USA
Middletown, DE
19 March 2022